ALSO BY MATTHEW PARKER

The Battle of Britain

MONTE
CASSINO

MONTE CASSINO

The Hardest-Fought Battle of World War II

Matthew Parker

DOUBLEDAY

New York   London   Toronto   Sydney   Auckland

PUBLISHED BY DOUBLEDAY
a division of Random House, Inc.

DOUBLEDAY and the portrayal of an anchor with a dolphin are
registered trademarks of Random House, Inc.

Library of Congress Cataloging-in-Publication Data
Parker, Matthew.
Monte Cassino : the hardest-fought battle of World
War II / Matthew Parker.—1st ed.
p.   cm.
Originally published: London : Headline, 2003.
Includes bibliographical references and index.
1. Cassino, Battle of, Cassino, Italy, 1944.   I. Title.

D763.I82M657   2004
940.54'215622—dc22   2003068778

ISBN 0-385-50985-5
Copyright © 2004 by Matthew Parker

PRINTED IN THE UNITED STATES OF AMERICA

June 2004
First Edition in the United States of America

1 3 5 7 9 10 8 6 4 2

For Hannah

Love conquers all

CONTENTS

PART ONE

Sicily to Cassino

PART TWO

The First Battle

CONTENTS

PART THREE

The Second Battle

PART FOUR

The Third Battle

PART FIVE

The Fourth Battle

FOREWORD

They are saying, "The Generals learnt their lesson in the last war.
There are going to be no wholesale slaughters." I ask, how is
victory possible except by wholesale slaughters?
—Evelyn Waugh, October 1939

War makes sense only in black-and-white. The Second World War has a unique position in popular memory as a "good war," particularly when compared with the First World War. Fought by the United Nations (as the Allies referred to themselves) against the tyranny of Nazism and the aggression of the Japanese, the victorious conclusion of the fighting ended many appalling crimes against humanity and justified all the sacrifices made by the men on the right side. Now, whenever the morality of a war is discussed, it is always measured against the yardstick of the Second World War. It has become the war that justifies war.

To a large extent, the Second World War has been written by its victors as a heroic narrative. For every *Catch-22* or *Slaughterhouse-Five*, there have been hundreds of novels, histories, and films celebrating the unshakeable moral certainties of the fighting. For my generation, growing up in the 1970s, the war films we were shown and the comics that seemed to be everywhere were all about the Second World War. It is impossible to imagine the popular conception of the First World War making an appropriate backdrop for such straightforward stories, just as war games played by young boys never involved the trenches or more recent, even more morally ambiguous conflicts. It was always us against the Nazis, good versus evil.

The First World War, as well as contributing to the causes of the Second, also shaped people's responses to it. At the beginning of the Second World War, it was hoped that new technologies would prevent the appalling attrition of infantrymen that occurred in the First. Interwar advances in aircraft, guns, tanks, submarines, and bombs led people to believe that, this time, the fighting would be fast-moving, mechanized, dominated by air power, somehow "remote-controlled," or carried out by a few experts. The popular story of the Battle of Britain—with scores of downed planes being chalked up on blackboards as if it were a cricket match—to an extent conforms to this pattern, and this view of the Second World War, at least in the West, as somehow "cleaner" than the First, has survived both the subsequent fighting and the postwar period.

The Battle of Monte Cassino throws all of this into question. Instead of fighting a battle of rapid movement, the men found themselves in scenes straight out of the Western Front in 1916–17. The terrain at Cassino sent the fighting back to a premechanized age. The mountains of central Italy and winter weather conspired to make technology such as armor useless. One hard-working mule was more prized than a dozen tanks, and the Allies' huge numerical advantage in artillery and aircraft was seldom decisive and often a hindrance. For one thing, such firepower had its risks. It has been estimated that a third of Allied casualties in Italy were caused by "friendly fire"; one American artilleryman at Cassino bemoaned that American bombers killed more of his division than did the Luftwaffe.

Nor was there much nationalistic certainty or unity of purpose driving the forces in Italy. With so many different national and ethnic groups from such radically different societies, it would have been an impossibility. As well as American and British soldiers, the Allied ranks included New Zealanders, Canadians, Nepalese, Indians, French, Belgians, South Africans, Tunisians, Algerians, Moroccans, Senegalese, Poles, Italians, and even Brazilians. Within these groups were units made up of Native Americans, Japanese-Americans, and Maoris. They were all there for different reasons. The result was a coalition riddled at the highest level with distrust and jealousy, with the inevitable consequences of misunderstandings and mistakes. In large part badly led and poorly equipped, the Allied soldiers who fought at Cassino could see from the way they were downgraded in the press at home that they were fighting battles of enormous scale and cost that were, at best, of secondary strategic importance, with the scant resources in reserves to match.

The Germans were even worse off. For every shell that Krupps sent over, General Motors sent back five. As well as artillery ammunition, the Germans were desperately short of basic food and clothing for the frontline troops guarding icy mountaintops in mid-winter. Many froze to death for lack of a greatcoat.

Between these opposing groups of men, in some places facing each other over just twenty or thirty yards of open ground, there was a shared suffering of the fighting and the elements, and surprisingly often the war would be stopped in local areas so that teams of stretcher bearers from both sides could work together to rescue the numerous wounded. Many record the bafflement of then resuming efforts to kill one another once the time of the truce was up.

From firsthand accounts, contemporary diaries and letters, and through listening to hundreds of veterans, a picture emerges of most people's experience of war that is different from the black-and-white image of popular conception. The men's descriptions of their times in action are dominated by confusion, fear, blunders, and accidents; they also talk about the times of boredom, of longing for home, the "chickenshit" or "bull" of the army as well as of the companionship with friends, many lost. They discuss how the experience changed them, and their feelings now about what happened.

While aiming to explain the strategic and tactical compromises and fudges that led to the battles, this book focuses on the human experience of the men there at the time, rather than playing "what if?" games or "weighing" the performance of the generals. To this end, I have tried as much as possible to let the eyewitnesses tell the story in their own words.

MAPS

The Monastery and the Gustav Line

Only the bloodbaths of Verdun and Passchendaele or the very worst of the Second World War fighting on the Eastern Front can compare to Monte Cassino. The largest land battle in Europe, Cassino was the bitterest and bloodiest of the Western Allies' struggles against the German Wehrmacht on any front of the Second World War. On the German side, many compared it unfavorably with Stalingrad.

After the conquest of Sicily, the invasion of Italy in 1943 saw Allied troops facing the German army in a lengthy campaign on the mainland of Europe for the first time for three years. By the beginning of 1944, Italy was still the Western Allies' only active front against Nazi-controlled Europe, and progress had been painfully slow. The campaign was becoming an embarrassment, and tensions between the Allies were rising.

It was not an easy task the Allies had set themselves. Not since Belisarius in A.D. 536 had anyone successfully taken Rome from the south. Hannibal even traversed the Alps rather than taking the direct route from Carthage. Napoleon is credited with saying, "Italy is a boot. You have to enter it from the top." The reason is the geography south of Rome. High mountains are bisected by fast-flowing rivers. The only possible route to the Italian capital from the south is up the old Via Casilina, now known as Route 6. Eighty miles south of Rome, this road passes up the valley of the Liri River. This was where the German commander, Kesselring, chose to make his stand. Towering over the entrance to the valley was the monastery of Monte Cassino.

It is one of Christianity's most sacred sites. Reportedly founded by the Roman nobleman Saint Benedict in 529, the abbey became the blueprint for monasteries in Western Europe. From Monte Cassino, Benedictine monks set out to establish monasteries throughout the Christian world. Meanwhile, the monastery's great library saw the preservation and copying of writings from antiquity onward, the safeguarding of the heritage of early civilization. The monastery was largely destroyed during an earthquake in 1349, but rebuilding started straightaway with the support of Pope Urban V. The new abbey was massive, a vast complex of buildings around five courtyards. It had walls twenty feet thick at their base; from below, the huge building, with its grim rows of cell windows, looked like a fortress. During the Renaissance the abbey became a favorite destination for pilgrims. The Benedictine monks, as was their custom, washed the travelers' feet and served them at the table. During one year in the early seventeenth century there were eighty thousand visitors. Generations of Italians labored to beautify the buildings. During the eighteenth century, in the hands of several of Italy's finest artists, the monastery became a baroque masterpiece and a center for the fine arts. In 1868 the abbey became Italian national property, but the library remained one of the most important in the world: By 1943 it contained over forty thousand manuscripts and much of the writings of Tacitus, Cicero, Horace, Virgil, Ovid, and many others. Over the gate of the monastery was carved one word: *Pax.*

But Benedict had chosen his site at a time when Christianity, based on Rome, was at its lowest ebb. To protect his new community, he had built his monastery on the top of more than five hundred meters of solid rock at the end of a mountain spur that rises almost vertically above the valleys beneath. From its high windows, one can see for miles around; all the approaches to the mountain are laid out to view like a map.

At the end of 1943 it was already considered one of the finest defensive positions in Europe and had been studied as such in Italian staff colleges for years. As well as benefiting from its commanding position, it was protected by the Rapido and Garigliano Rivers, which form a natural moat in front of it. Its flanks are guarded by jagged, trackless mountains: from the Liri valley almost to the coast stretch the Aurunci Mountains; behind the monastery the Cassino Massif rises into the forbidding Abruzzi Range.